CAN'T I JUST
HELP MY KID PICK A PATH?
A Career + College Survival Guide for Parents Who Want to Get It Right

Jennifer Larsen

Originality Statement

This book is an original work written by the author and reflects their unique ideas, voice, and instructional approach. While it may reference common educational and career-planning concepts, all content, including structure, language, exercises, and framework, is the author's own creation. Any similarities to other published works are purely coincidental.

Printed in the United States of America

ISBN: 979-8-9987626-6-6

First Edition

Cover design by Rachel Bostwick

Interior design and layout by Rachel Bostwick

For information or bulk orders, visit cantijust.com

CAN'T I JUST HELP MY KID PICK A PATH?
A Career + College Survival Guide for Parents Who Want to Get It Right

📖 Introduction:
Success Without College

◆ **Helping Your Teen Navigate Their Future – Without the Pressure**

If you're reading this, you're probably **trying to help your teenager figure out what comes next.**

✓ Maybe they have **no idea what they want to do.**

✓ Maybe they have **too many ideas.**

✓ Or maybe they're convinced they'll just **"figure it out later."**

Meanwhile, you're over here thinking,

❓ *How do I help without pushing too hard?*

❓ *How do I guide them without overwhelming them?*

❓ *What if they make the wrong choice and regret it later?*

You're **not alone.** And if it feels harder to guide a teen into a **solid career path** than it was when we were their age, that's because **it is.**

◆ **Why Career Planning Feels Harder Today**

When we were growing up, the **path was more straightforward** for most people. There were **fewer career options, clearer job expectations, and college was far more affordable.**

Today, the world is different:

- ✓ **There are more career choices than ever,** but that also makes deciding harder.

- ✓ **College is expensive,** and many degrees don't guarantee high-paying jobs.

- ✓ **Teens feel pressure to "figure it all out" quickly,** even though most careers evolve over time.

- ✓ **The job market is unpredictable,** with automation, AI, and new industries constantly changing what's in demand.

And let's be honest – **teens don't always take advice well,** especially when it comes from their parents.

But here's the good news: **You don't need to have all the answers.** What your teen really needs is **support, encouragement, and someone who helps them ask the right questions.**

That's where this book comes in.

◆ **How This Guide Will Help You (Without Adding Stress)**

Your teen's main book is **designed to help them explore their strengths, interests, and career options.** But they'll get **so much more out of it if you're involved.**

◆ **Example:** Imagine your teen is trying to decide on an after-school activity. You could tell them **what to do** – or you could ask them:

> ✓ *"Would you rather do something hands-on or creative?"*
>
> ✓ *"Do you like working in a team or independently?"*
>
> ✓ *"What's something you've always been curious about but never tried?"*

The same strategy works for **career conversations.** Instead of pressuring them to "decide," you can **help them explore in a way that feels natural and low-stakes.**

◆ **How to Support Without Overstepping**

You don't have to **sit down and do assignments together** (unless you want to), but **a little engagement on your part can go a long way.**

Here's how you can help:

- ✓ **Ask, don't dictate.** Instead of telling them what they should do, **ask what excites them, what they're curious about, and what skills they think they have.**

- ✓ **Encourage self-reflection.** Teens often **overlook their own strengths.** Help them recognize what they do well – even things they don't see as "skills."

- ✓ **Be open to different paths.** College is **great,** but it's not the only route to success. **Careers come in many forms, and fulfillment matters just as much as financial security.**

- ✓ **Use this book as a conversation starter.** Ask about their thoughts on each section. *What surprised them? What ideas are standing out?*

◀ **Example:** If your teen is **great at problem-solving**, they might not realize that skill can be applied to **engineering, business, cybersecurity, or even event planning.** Helping them connect the dots **expands their career possibilities.**

Most importantly, **remind them that they don't have to figure it all out at once.** The goal isn't to **lock in a lifetime decision at 17** – it's to build a mindset that helps them **adapt, explore, and make informed choices along the way.**

☑ **Key Takeaway:** Your teen doesn't need a **perfect plan.** They just need **curiosity, confidence, and the freedom to explore without fear.**

◆ You're Already Doing Something Right

By reading this, you've already shown that you **care deeply about your teen's future.** That alone makes a huge difference.

◆ Reminder for Parents:

- ✓ **You don't need to be a career expert** – you just need to be **a supportive guide.**
- ✓ **Your teen doesn't need all the answers today.** Career paths evolve over time.
- ✓ **Your role is to help them explore, not pressure them into a decision.**

Key Takeaway: You're not here to make choices **for them** – you're here to help them **discover what works for them.**

◆ **What's Next?**

In the next sections, we'll talk about:

✓ **How to understand your teen's perspective** (so they feel heard, not pressured).

✓ **How to have career conversations that open doors instead of shutting them down.**

✓ **How to support their exploration without micromanaging.**

◆ **Up Next: Understanding Your Teen's Perspective.**

📖 Section 1: Understanding Your Teen's Perspective

Helping your teen figure out their future can feel like a **daunting task** – especially when they seem **uninterested, overwhelmed, or unsure of where to start.** The truth is, most teens **don't have a clear picture of their future yet**, and that's **completely normal.**

Your role as a parent **isn't to hand them a fully mapped-out plan**, but to help them **start asking the right questions, exploring possibilities, and building the confidence to make decisions at their own pace.**

◆ Why Teens Struggle with Career Decisions

If you've ever asked your teen, **"What do you want to do when you grow up?"** and been met with a **shrug**, you're not alone. Today's teens face a world that's **very different from the one we grew up in.**

Some of the biggest challenges they face include:

◆ 1. Too Many Choices, Not Enough Direction

When we were growing up, career paths seemed **simpler and more structured.** You went to college, learned a trade, or got a job and worked your way up. Today's teens have **more career options than ever** – but instead of making things easier, this often leads to **decision paralysis.**

◆ **Example:** A teen who enjoys technology might feel overwhelmed by the choices:

  ✓ Should they go into **coding, game design, cybersecurity, or IT support?**

  ✓ Should they **attend college, enroll in a bootcamp, or get a certification instead?**

  ✓ Will they make **the wrong choice and regret it later?**

☑ **How Parents Can Help:** Instead of asking **"What do you want to do?"**, help them **narrow their options** by focusing on their interests, skills, and long-term goals.

✦ **Better Questions to Ask:**

> ✓ *"What kinds of problems do you like solving?"*
>
> ✓ *"Would you rather work with people, technology, or ideas?"*
>
> ✓ *"What's something you'd love to learn more about?"*

✦ **2. Pressure to "Get It Right" the First Time**

Many teens believe that **their first career choice is permanent** – that if they don't pick the "perfect" path now, they'll be stuck.

✓ They hear messages like **"Choose wisely or you'll be paying for it forever"** (especially with the high cost of college).

✓ They see adults who **regret their career choices** and fear making the same mistake.

✓ They worry that **switching careers later means failure.**

🔹 **Example:** A teen who loves art but worries they won't make enough money might feel stuck between:

> ✓ **Pursuing a passion** (graphic design, animation, illustration)

> ✓ **Choosing a "safe" degree** (business, marketing, or computer science)

> ✓ **Feeling paralyzed** because they don't want to make the wrong choice

☑ **How Parents Can Help:** Remind them that **careers are not set in stone.** Many people **change fields multiple times**, and most skills **transfer between industries.**

🔹 **Better Ways to Phrase It:**

✗ *"You need to pick a stable career and stick with it."*

✓ **Instead, try:** "Your first job doesn't have to be your forever job. It's okay to try different things and adjust along the way."

🔹 **3. Limited Real-World Experience**

Many teens have **only been exposed to a handful of careers** – usually those of their parents, teachers, or professionals they've seen on TV. **Without firsthand experience, it's hard to know what different jobs are really like.**

🔹 **Example:**

- A teen who **likes science** may assume **"doctor" is their only option** – but they might love careers in **forensic science, biotech, or lab research.**

- A teen interested in **fashion** might not realize that the industry includes **marketing, product development, styling, and costume design.**

☑ **How Parents Can Help:**

> ✓ **Encourage career exposure** through job shadowing, volunteer work, or internships.

✓ **Introduce them to professionals** in different fields for informational interviews.

✓ **Suggest online research** – many careers have free resources, webinars, or "day in the life" videos.

◆ **Better Ways to Phrase It:**

✗ *"You need to decide what you want to do right now."*

✓ **Instead, try:** "You don't have to commit today – let's explore a few careers and see what interests you."

◆ **4. Conflicting Messages About What They "Should" Do**

Parents, teachers, social media, and society send mixed signals:

✓ **Follow your passion!**

✓ **Be practical!**

✓ **College is essential!**

✓ **Trade schools are better!**

✓ **Work for yourself!**

✓ **Work for stability!**

No wonder teens feel stuck. They're bombarded with advice that often **contradicts itself.**

◆ **Example:** A teen might hear:

- **From school counselors:** "Go to college – it's the best path."

- **From social media influencers:** "Skip college, start a business instead."

- **From parents:** "Just pick something stable and don't waste time."

How Parents Can Help:

✓ Instead of telling them **what they should do**, ask **what makes sense for them.**

✓ Guide them to **weigh the pros and cons** of different career paths.

✓ Remind them that **success looks different for everyone.**

Better Ways to Phrase It:

✗ *"You have to go to college to be successful."*

✓ **Instead, try:** "College is one option, but there are many ways to build a great career. Let's look at what makes the most sense for you."

◆ **The Balance Between Financial Security and Fulfillment**

One of the biggest conflicts parents and teens face is the **classic debate:**

✓ **Should they do what they love?**

✓ **Or should they focus on what makes money?**

Parents **want their kids to be financially secure,** and **teens want careers that excite them.** But the truth is, **these don't have to be opposites.**

☑ **How to Find the Middle Ground:**

  ✓ **Help your teen find careers that combine what they enjoy and what's in demand.**

  ✓ **Encourage skill-building.** Many careers **pay well if you develop specialized skills.**

  ✓ **Remind them that careers evolve.** Their first job won't define their whole life.

◆ **Better Ways to Phrase It:**

✗ *"You'll never make money doing that."*

✓ **Instead, try:** "Let's look at different ways you can turn your interests into a career that supports you."

❖ **What's Next?**

Now that we've covered **why career planning can be overwhelming for teens,** the next step is learning how to **talk about it in a way that helps rather than pressures them.**

In **Section 2**, we'll discuss:

  ✓ **How to ask career questions without making them feel judged.**

  ✓ **How to keep career conversations open and productive.**

  ✓ **Common mistakes parents make — and what to say instead.**

➤ **Up Next: Conversations That Help (and Ones That Hurt).**

📖 Section 2: Conversations That Help (and Ones That Hurt)

Talking to your teen about their future can feel like **walking a tightrope.**

✓ Say **too much,** and they shut down.

✓ Say **too little,** and they might drift without direction.

The key is asking the **right questions, listening more than advising,** and creating a space where they feel comfortable **exploring ideas — without fear of judgment or pressure.**

This section will help you **have more productive conversations** while avoiding common pitfalls that can make teens feel **pressured, discouraged, or misunderstood.**

◆ **How to Ask Questions That Spark Interest**

One of the best ways to guide your teen is to **help them think**, rather than **telling them what to do.**

✓ **Shift from** *"What do you want to do?"*

✓ **To:** *"What do you enjoy doing?"*

Many teens struggle with **career labels** but can easily talk about their **interests and strengths.** Instead of asking them to name a job, ask about:

✓ **Activities they enjoy** (creating, fixing things, helping people, organizing, analyzing, etc.).

✓ **Subjects or hobbies that interest them** (science, technology, sports, media, business, design, etc.).

✓ **Situations where they naturally excel** (leading, problem-solving, staying focused, working with their hands, etc.).

◆ **Example Parent-Teen Conversations**

✗ **Parent:** "You need to start thinking about your future. What do you want to do?"

✗ **Teen:** *[Shrugs]* "I don't know."

✗ **Parent:** "Well, you have to choose something! You can't just wait forever."

⊖ *Why this doesn't work:* It puts **pressure on them** without giving them a starting point.

✓ Better Approach:

- **✓ Parent:** "You don't have to know your exact career yet, but let's start with something easier – what kinds of things do you enjoy working on?"

- **✓ Teen:** "I like figuring out how things work."

- **✓ Parent:** "That's great! Some careers focus on problem-solving – engineering, coding, even forensic science. Want to explore a few of those?"

Why this works: Instead of demanding an answer, it **helps them reflect** and **explore possibilities.**

◆ **How to Point Out Strengths Without Sounding Like You're Pushing**

Sometimes, **teens don't see their own strengths** because they assume:

✓ *"It's easy for me, so it must not be a real skill."*

✓ *"I just like doing it – I never thought of it as a career."*

◆ **Example:** A teen who **loves organizing things** may not realize that could lead to careers in **event planning, logistics, or operations management.**

How to naturally introduce career possibilities without making it feel forced:

✓ **Parent:** "You're really great at organizing things. Have you ever thought about careers where that could be useful?"

✓ **Teen:** "Like what?"

✓ **Parent:** "Well, event planners, project managers, and even film producers need those skills. Want to check out how those jobs work?"

☑ *Why this works:* It introduces career ideas **without forcing them into a decision.**

◆ Common Pitfalls That Shut Down Career Conversations

Even well-intended advice can accidentally make your teen **shut down or feel pressured.** Here are some phrases to avoid — and **better alternatives.**

✗ **"You'll never make money doing that."**

✓ **Instead, try:** "That's an interesting field. Have you looked into the different career paths related to it?"

◆ **Why?** Even careers that seem impractical often have **profitable niches.** Instead of shutting them down, help them explore **options within their interests.**

◆ **Example:** If your teen loves **writing**, don't dismiss it as "impractical." Instead, explore **high-paying writing careers** like **technical writing, copywriting, UX writing, or publishing.**

✗ **"Just go to college and figure it out later."**

✓ **Instead, try:** "College is one option, but let's think about what you actually want to do first."

◆ **Why?** College is a **huge investment**, and going in without a plan can lead to **wasted time and money.** Encourage them to **explore careers before committing to a degree.**

◆ **Better Approach:**
> ✓ **Parent:** "If college is part of your plan, let's check which careers require a degree and which don't. That way, you can make a smart choice about your education."

✕ **"I know what's best for you."**

✓ **Instead, try:** "I want to help you find a path that makes sense for you. Let's figure it out together."

✦ **Why?** Even if you have valuable insights, teens need to feel like they have **control over their own future.**

✦ **Example:**

 ✓ Instead of saying, *"You should go into business because it's safe,"*

 ✓ Try, *"You seem interested in leadership and strategy – have you thought about business or marketing?"*

☑ *Why this works:* It presents career ideas **without making them feel forced into a path.**

◆ How to Keep the Conversation Open and Supportive

◆ 1. Listen More Than You Speak

If your teen is willing to **talk about their future,** resist the urge to **jump in with advice too quickly.** Sometimes, they just need to **talk it out first.**

> ✓ Let them **express their thoughts** before offering input.
>
> ✓ Ask **follow-up questions** instead of giving immediate solutions.

◆ 2. Be Patient with Uncertainty

It's okay if they **don't have a clear answer yet.** Encourage them to:

> ✓ Try **different experiences** (internships, courses, job shadowing).
>
> ✓ Explore **multiple career options** instead of locking into one path.

◆ Example:

✓ Instead of saying, *"You need to decide already,"*

✓ Try, *"It's okay if you're still figuring things out. Let's find ways for you to explore different careers before making a decision."*

✦ 3. Check In Periodically, Not Just Once

Career exploration **isn't a one-time conversation** – it's an **ongoing process.**

✓ Keep the dialogue open by **checking in casually** rather than having **one big pressure-filled talk.**

✦ **Example:** Instead of, *"We need to have a serious talk about your future,"*

   ✓ Try bringing it up **naturally in everyday situations**, like:

   ✓ *"I saw an article about someone who turned their love of gaming into a career – want to check it out?"*

   ✓ *"I just met someone who works in cybersecurity – want to hear what they said about their job?"*

☑ *Why this works:* **Low-pressure conversations** keep career discussions **open and ongoing.**

◆ **What's Next?**

Even with open, productive conversations, some teens **still feel anxious about making career choices.** The pressure to **"get it right"** can make them feel **paralyzed or uncertain.**

In the next section, we'll discuss:

> ✓ **Why career anxiety is so common for teens today.**
>
> ✓ **How to support a teen who's feeling overwhelmed.**
>
> ✓ **Ways to help them move forward, even if they're afraid of making the wrong choice.**

◆ **Up Next: Handling Teen Anxiety About Career Choices.**

📖 Section 3:
Handling Teen
Anxiety About Career Choices

◆ **Why Career Anxiety is So Common for Teens**

If your teen is feeling **overwhelmed, stuck, or even avoiding career conversations altogether**, you're not alone. Career anxiety is **more common than ever** because today's teens are facing:

✓ **More choices than ever before** – The sheer number of career paths can lead to **decision paralysis.**

✓ **Pressure to make the "right" choice immediately** – Teens feel like they have to **pick a lifelong career** at 17.

✓ **Fear of failure** – They're afraid of **choosing wrong** and ending up unhappy or unsuccessful.

✓ **Social comparison** – Social media makes it easy to compare their progress to peers who seem to have it all figured out.

✓ **Worries about money** – Rising college costs and student loan debt make career decisions feel **high-stakes.**

Many parents see this anxiety as a lack of motivation – but it's often the opposite. Some teens shut down because they **care so much about making the right choice that they're afraid to choose anything.**

☑ **Key Takeaway:** If your teen is struggling with career anxiety, they don't need **pressure to decide – they need reassurance that they can explore, test, and change paths as they grow.**

◆ **Signs Your Teen is Struggling with Career Anxiety**

Some teens **talk openly about their fears,** but others **keep them bottled up.** Watch for these common signs of career-related stress:

✦ **Signs of Career Anxiety:**

  ✕ **Avoids career discussions** – Changes the subject or shrugs off questions about the future.

  ✕ **Feels paralyzed by indecision** – Says, *"I don't know,"* but also avoids exploring options.

  ✕ **Expresses fear of failure** – Worries about *"picking the wrong career"* or *"ruining their life"* with one bad choice.

  ✕ **Compares themselves to others** – Feels behind because *"everyone else knows what they're doing."*

  ✕ **Obsesses over the "perfect" choice** – Won't commit to anything because they think there's *one right answer.*

✦ **Example:** A teen who **loves writing** might feel anxious because they've heard **"writers don't make money."** Instead of exploring related careers (journalism, marketing, UX writing), they **shut down** because they think their interests won't lead to success.

▧ **Key Takeaway:** Career anxiety **isn't about laziness – it's about fear of making the wrong choice.** Your teen may need **encouragement, perspective, and real-world exposure** to move past these fears.

◆ **How to Help an Anxious Teen Navigate Career Choices**

If your teen is feeling overwhelmed, here's how to **help them move forward without pressure:**

- ✓ **Normalize Uncertainty** – Let them know that **most adults don't have everything figured out either.**

- ✓ **Encourage Small Steps Instead of Big Decisions** – Career choices aren't **all or nothing.** They can **test different options through internships, part-time work, or courses.**

- ✓ **Expose Them to Career Possibilities** – Sometimes, anxiety comes from **not knowing what's out there.** Help them explore jobs through **shadowing, networking, or career fairs.**

- ✓ **Help Them Separate Interests from Careers** – If they love something but don't see a career path, help them **connect the dots** to industries that use those skills.

◆ **Example Conversations:**

Teen: "I have no idea what I want to do."

Parent: "That's totally okay. Most people don't figure it out right away. What's something you've been curious about?"

Teen: "I don't want to pick the wrong career."

Parent: "No career choice is permanent. Plenty of people switch paths over time. Let's look at careers where your skills can transfer."

Teen: "I don't know how to choose between all these options."

Parent: "Let's break it down. What's something you'd actually enjoy learning more about?"

◆ **Final Thought: Career Anxiety Fades with Action**

The best way to **ease career anxiety** is to **take small steps.** Your teen doesn't have to **choose today** – they just need to **start exploring.**

☑ **Encourage curiosity over commitment.**

☑ **Remind them that careers evolve over time.**

☑ **Help them focus on next steps, not final answers.**

◆ **What's Next?**

Now that we've covered **why career anxiety is common and how to help your teen move past fear,** the next step is ensuring they engage with their career guide in a way that feels **helpful, not overwhelming.**

◆ **Up Next: How to Help Your Teen Use the Main Book.**

📖 Section 4:
How to Help Your Teen Use the Main Book

Even the **best career guidance book** won't be useful if it just **sits on a shelf.**
But let's be honest – most teens **aren't going to eagerly dive into a self-re-flection workbook on their own.**

That's where you come in.

Your role **isn't to make them do every exercise** or treat this like another
school assignment. Instead, it's about **helping them engage with the book** in
a way that feels **natural, useful, and even – dare we say – interesting.**

- **How to Get Them Started (Without Forcing It)**

If you push too hard, your teen might **resist engaging** with the book. Instead,
try these strategies to make the process **feel natural.**

1. Give Them Space to Explore on Their Own First

Some teens will **resist anything that feels like a "parent-led" project.** In-stead of presenting this as a **must-do task,** keep it casual.

Example:

✓ Instead of, *"You need to read this book and do the exercises,"*

✓ Try, *"I found this book and thought it might help. No pressure, but if you
check it out, I'd love to hear what you think."*

Why this works: This approach makes them **feel in control** rather than feeling
like it's another assignment.

2. Make It a Conversation, Not an Assignment

Instead of **asking whether they've "done the exercises",** use the book as a
jumping-off point for discussions.

✦ Example:

✓ **Parent:** "I was flipping through the book and found the section on strengths really interesting. What did you think?"

✓ **Teen:** "I haven't looked at it yet."

✓ **Parent:** "No worries! One of the questions was about skills you don't even realize you have. I was thinking about mine – want to guess what they are?"

Why this works: It **keeps the conversation casual** while sparking curiosity.

✦ 3. Share Your Own Experiences

Teens often resist career conversations because they feel like **they're the only ones struggling.** Sharing **your own career journey** can make them feel **less pressured** and more willing to explore.

✦ Example Parent Dialogue:

✓ **Parent:** "When I was your age, I had no idea what I wanted to do. I picked a major just because I thought it was practical, but later realized I actually loved something else."

✓ **Teen:** "Really? What did you switch to?"

✓ **Parent:** "Marketing! I started in finance, but I realized I loved the creative side of business more. I wish I had explored my options earlier."

Why this works: It shows that **career paths aren't set in stone** and that **exploration is normal.**

◆ Ways to Keep Your Teen Engaged with the Book

If your teen starts using the book but **loses interest**, here are **ways to keep them engaged.**

◆ 1. Tie the Book to Real-Life Experiences

Teens will be **more motivated** to explore careers when they see **real-world connections.**

◆ Example:

✓ If they're interested in **sports**, show them careers beyond being an athlete, like **sports management, physical therapy, or coaching.**

✓ If they enjoy **gaming**, introduce careers in **game design, coding, or streaming.**

How to connect the book to real life:

✓ If they read about a career that **sparks interest,** look up **day-in-the-life videos** on YouTube.

✓ If they complete a **strengths or interests exercise**, brainstorm **careers that align with their results.**

◆ 2. Turn It into a Fun Challenge

If your teen is **reluctant to do the exercises**, turn them into a **friendly game.**

◆ Example:

✓ **Parent:** "Let's both do the 'Hidden Skills' exercise and compare answers – want to see if we come up with the same ones for you?"

✓ **Teen:** "Okay, but only if I get to guess yours too."

☑ *Why this works:* It **removes the pressure** and makes it feel **interactive.**

◆ **3. Celebrate Small Wins, Not Just the Final Answer**

Teens don't have to **figure out their entire future overnight.** Encourage **small steps** and celebrate their progress.

◆ **Example:**

✓ Instead of asking, *"Have you picked a career yet?"*

✓ Say, *"You've been exploring different fields – what's something new you've learned about yourself?"*

☑ *Why this works:* It shifts the focus from **pressure to progress.**

◆ What If They Seem Uninterested?

Not every teen will **immediately engage** with the book, and that's okay. Here's what **not to do** – and what to try instead.

✕ Don't: Nag or Force a Schedule

✓ **Instead, try:** Leaving the book accessible and casually checking in.

◆ **Example:** *"I know you're busy, but if you ever want to look at that career book, it's on the table."*

✕ Don't: Dismiss Their Resistance

✓ **Instead, try:** Asking why they're hesitant.

◆ **Example:**

   ✓ **Parent:** "I noticed you haven't looked at the book yet – does something about it feel unhelpful?"

   ✓ **Teen:** "I just don't know where to start."

   ✓ **Parent:** "That's totally fair. Want to go through one part together?"

✕ Don't: Make It a High-Stakes Discussion

✓ **Instead, try:** Keeping it **low-pressure and natural.**

◆ **Example:**

      ✓ Instead of, *"You need to decide your future,"*

      ✓ Try, *"No rush, but I'd love to hear what's interesting to you so far."*

☑ *Why this works:* It keeps **career exploration light and approachable.**

◆ Making This a Team Effort

Some teens **may not dive into the book on their own** – but they might be **more interested** if they see you participating.

◆ Ways to Make It a Shared Experience:

- √ **Try an exercise yourself first.** Fill out one of the self-reflection questions and share your answers.

- √ **Discuss topics over a casual meal.** Ask open-ended questions about the book's concepts.

- √ **Use it to spark outside activities.** If your teen reads about a career they like, suggest a job shadowing opportunity or a related project.

◆ Example Parent Dialogue:

- √ **Parent:** "I just did the 'What Skills Do You Have?' exercise. Turns out, I'm good at explaining things – maybe I should have been a teacher!"

- √ **Teen:** "Really? I never thought about that for you."

- √ **Parent:** "Yeah! Want to take a look and see what skills you might not realize you have?"

Why this works: It makes the book **interactive and engaging**, rather than a solo task.

◆ What's Next?

The more your teen **engages with career exploration,** the better they'll under-stand **themselves and their options.**

But beyond the book, **there's another key factor in making great career choices — real-world exposure.**

✦ **Up Next: Exposing Your Teen to Real-World Career Options.**

📖 Section 5:
Exposing Your Teen
to Real-World Career Options

No matter how many career books, personality tests, or interest surveys your teen completes, **nothing replaces real-world experience.**

The best way to help them make **informed career choices** is to expose them to as many **different experiences as possible** – giving them a chance to see what they enjoy, what they're naturally good at, and what feels right for them.

Think of it like **introducing a child to different foods.** You don't expect them to love everything they try, but the more they're exposed to, the better they understand their preferences. **The same goes for careers** – the more they experience, the more confidently they can choose.

◆ **Why Career Exposure Matters**

Many teens **only have a vague idea** of what careers actually involve. They might say they want to be a **lawyer, doctor, or engineer** because those are familiar job titles – but do they really know **what a day in those jobs looks like?**

◆ **How Exposure Helps Your Teen:**

✓ **Seeing a career in action is different from reading about it.** A teen might think they want to work in a hospital, but after shadowing a nurse, they realize they **can't stand the sight of blood.** Or they might not consider engineering, but after visiting a robotics lab, they **discover a passion for design.**

✓ **It helps them discover what they love (and what they don't).** Exposure isn't just about finding the **right** career – it's also about eliminating options that **don't** fit. The earlier they figure that out, the fewer detours they'll take later.

✓ **It makes career decisions feel less abstract.** Many teens struggle to answer *"What do you want to do?"* because they don't have enough context to make an informed decision. Giving them **hands-on experiences** turns vague ideas into real possibilities.

- **Ways to Give Your Teen Career Exposure**

You don't have to **orchestrate grand experiences** – sometimes, the best insights come from small, everyday opportunities.

Here are **practical ways** to help your teen explore careers in a way that feels **natural and engaging.**

1. Encourage Job Shadowing

A few hours **watching someone work** can provide **valuable insight** into what a job is really like.

Example:

- ✓ A teen interested in **medicine** might shadow a **doctor, nurse, or EMT.**
- ✓ A teen drawn to **law** could spend a day with a **paralegal or courtroom assistant.**
- ✓ A **tech-focused teen** might observe an **IT specialist or software developer.**

How Parents Can Help:

- ✓ Ask **friends, family, or local businesses** if they'd allow your teen to shadow for a day.
- ✓ Check if **high schools or career centers** offer shadowing programs.
- ✓ Encourage your teen to **reach out on their own** – learning to network is a valuable skill!

Example Parent-Teen Dialogue:

- ✓ **Parent:** "I know you've been interested in marketing. Would you want to shadow my coworker who does social media management?"

✓ **Teen:** "Maybe. What do they do?"

✓ **Parent:** "They handle brand accounts, run ad campaigns, and create content. It might be a good way to see if that side of business interests you."

Why this works: It introduces **career exposure naturally** and gives the teen **a choice.**

✦ 2. Help Them Find Internships or Part-Time Jobs

Even if it's **not their dream job**, working in different environments **teaches valuable skills.**

✦ **Example:**

✓ **Retail or food service jobs** teach **customer service, teamwork, and problem-solving.**

✓ **Office jobs** expose teens to **business operations, scheduling, and communication.**

✓ **Internships (paid or unpaid)** provide **real-world industry experience.**

☑ How Parents Can Help:

✓ Check **local businesses, community programs, and school counselors** for opportunities.

✓ Help them **write a simple email** to ask about openings.

✓ Encourage them to **start small** – even short-term work experience is beneficial.

✦ Example Parent-Teen Dialogue:

✓ **Teen:** "I don't want to work in fast food forever."

✓ **Parent:** "I get that. But having a job teaches responsibility. Plus, customer service skills are useful in almost every career."

✓ **Teen:** "Like how?"

✓ **Parent:** "Even if you become a doctor or business owner, you'll still need to communicate well with people. It's all connected."

☑ *Why this works:* It **reframes work experience as valuable,** even if it's not the teen's dream job.

✦ 3. Visit Different Workplaces

If you have the chance, take your teen to **a variety of work environments** – places they might not otherwise see.

✦ Examples of Workplaces to Visit:

✓ **A hospital or medical center** – Great for teens considering **healthcare careers.**

✓ **A news station or creative agency** – Helps teens see jobs in **media, marketing, and journalism.**

✓ **A construction site or manufacturing plant** – Ideal for those interested in **engineering, trades, or industrial work.**

✓ **A courtroom** – Gives insight into **legal and government careers.**

How Parents Can Help:

✓ If you have a **"Take Your Child to Work Day"**, use it as an opportunity!

✓ Call local businesses and ask if they **offer student tours.**

✓ Attend **career fairs or job expos** with them.

Example Parent-Teen Dialogue:

✓ **Parent:** "There's a tech company nearby that's doing an open house next week. Want to check it out?"

✓ **Teen:** "What would I even do there?"

✓ **Parent:** "Meet some employees, see how they work, and maybe get ideas for future careers. No pressure, just an opportunity to explore."

Why this works: It keeps career exploration **low-pressure and interactive.**

4. Encourage Hands-On Hobbies

Sometimes, hobbies reveal **hidden career paths.**

Examples of Hobbies That Connect to Careers:

✓ **Video editing** → Digital marketing, film production, YouTube content creation

✓ **Coding games for fun** → Software development, cybersecurity, game design

✓ **Fixing cars** → Mechanical engineering, auto repair, racing industry

✓ **Organizing school events** → Event planning, project management, hospitality

CAN'T I JUST HELP MY KID PICK A PATH?

☑ **How Parents Can Help:**

✓ Support **projects, clubs, or competitions** related to their interests.

✓ Encourage **side gigs** – selling art, designing websites, tutoring, etc.

✓ Help them connect **passions to potential career fields.**

◆ **Example Parent-Teen Dialogue:**

✓ **Parent:** "I noticed you've been editing videos for fun. Did you know video editing is a career?"

✓ **Teen:** "Really? I just do it for fun."

✓ **Parent:** "Lots of industries need video editors – marketing, social media, even film production. Want to check out what it takes to go pro?"

☑ *Why this works:* It helps teens see **their natural interests as potential career paths.**

◆ **Final Thought: Exposure Makes Career Choices Easier**

The more **careers your teen experiences firsthand**, the easier it will be for them to **decide what feels right.**

◆ **How Parents Can Support Career Exploration:**

✓ Encourage **curiosity over commitment.**

✓ Provide **exposure without pressure.**

✓ Celebrate **every step forward — even small ones.**

◆ **What's Next?**

Exposure is one of the best tools for career discovery, but what comes next?

In the next section, we'll talk about how to help your teen **sort through their experiences and make choices** – without overwhelming them or rushing the process.

◆ **Up Next: College, Trade School, or Straight to Work?**

📖 Section 6:
College, Trade School, or Straight to Work?

For a long time, the path after high school seemed **simple**:

✓ Go to college.

✓ Get a degree.

✓ Get a job.

But today, it's **not so clear-cut.**

✓ **College is more expensive than ever.** Parents and teens are rightfully concerned about student debt and whether a degree will actually **pay off.**

✓ **Skilled trades and alternative paths are gaining recognition.** Many high-paying jobs **don't require a four-year degree.**

✓ **The job market is unpredictable.** Some degrees **lead directly to careers**, while others don't. Meanwhile, **new industries are emerging all the time.**

With all these factors, it's no wonder teens feel **overwhelmed** by the choice.

Your role as a parent **isn't to decide for them** but to help them **weigh their options in a way that fits their strengths, interests, and goals.**

◆ **Understanding the Options (Without Bias)**

Each path has **pros and cons**, and what works for one teen **may not work for another.**

Here's a **balanced breakdown** of each option:

◆ **1. College (2-Year or 4-Year Degree)**

Best for:

- ✓ Careers that **require** specialized education (**medicine, law, engineering, teaching**).
- ✓ Those who enjoy **academic learning** and want the **structured college experience.**
- ✓ Fields where a degree is **required for career advancement.**

Financial Considerations:

- ✓ Private colleges **can be expensive,** but some offer **more financial aid.**
- ✓ In-state public universities **tend to be more affordable** than out-of-state options.
- ✓ Community college **can be a smart first step** before transferring to a four-year school.

⚠ Potential Downsides:

✓ Not all degrees lead directly to **high-paying jobs.**

✓ Many students **graduate with debt** but without clear career direction.

✓ Some careers require **more than just a degree** – internships, networking, and hands-on experience are just as important.

✦ Example:

✓ A student who loves **science** and wants to be a **physical therapist** would likely need **a college degree + graduate school.**

✓ A student who enjoys **business** might not need a degree if they focus on **entrepreneurship or certifications.**

☑ Parent Discussion Idea:

✓ Instead of saying, *"You have to go to college,"*

✓ Try, *"Let's research which careers actually require a degree and which don't."*

✦ 2. Trade Schools & Apprenticeships

✂ Best for:

✓ Hands-on learners who prefer **practical, skills-based work.**

✓ High-demand fields like **electricians, mechanics, plumbing, HVAC, welding, IT technicians.**

✓ Students who want to **start earning quickly** without a four-year commitment.

💰 Financial Considerations:

✓ Trade schools **cost significantly less** than college.

✓ Many apprenticeship programs **pay students while they learn.**

✓ Skilled trades often have **high job security and good salaries.**

⚠ Potential Downsides:

✓ Some trades require **physical labor or location-based work.**

✓ Fewer career shifts than a broad college degree might allow.

✦ Example:

✓ A teen who enjoys **fixing cars and working with their hands** might thrive as an **auto mechanic or machinist.**

✓ A student who loves **technology** but doesn't want a traditional college route could explore **cybersecurity or IT certifications.**

☑ Parent Discussion Idea:

✓ Instead of saying, *"College is the only way to make money,"*

✓ Try, *"Let's check out salary data for trade jobs vs. college degrees and compare earning potential."*

3. Straight to Work (Entry-Level Jobs & On-the-Job Training)

Best for:

✓ Teens who want to **gain work experience immediately** and explore careers through employment.

✓ Industries that offer **growth opportunities without a degree** (sales, tech, marketing, real estate).

✓ Those who plan to **earn and save before deciding on college or training.**

Financial Considerations:

✓ Immediate income with **no student debt.**

✓ Some companies offer **tuition reimbursement** for future education.

✓ Can allow time to **test different career paths before committing.**

Potential Downsides:

✓ Some entry-level jobs **don't pay well at first.**

✓ Career growth may be **slower without specialized training or education.**

Example:

✓ A teen unsure about their future could **work in customer service or retail** while exploring interests.

✓ A student who's great at **persuasion and people skills** might go straight into **sales or real estate.**

Parent Discussion Idea:

✓ Instead of saying, *"You need to pick a career before graduating,"*

✓ Try, *"If you're unsure, let's explore jobs that help you gain skills while figuring things out."*

◆ **How to Help Your Teen Choose (Without Pushing One Way)**

It's easy to default to our own views on **education and career paths,** but the best approach is to **help your teen consider the facts.**

◆ **1. Ask About Their Long-Term Goals**

✓ Instead of **pushing a decision**, guide them to think about the future.

◆ **Example Parent Dialogue:**

✓ **Parent:** "What kind of work sounds fulfilling to you?"

✓ **Teen:** "I like working with technology."

✓ **Parent:** "Great! Let's look at tech careers that require a degree vs. those that don't."

◆ **2. Research Career Salaries and Job Demand Together**

✓ Show them how to compare **career salaries, job openings, and education requirements.**

◆ **Example:**

✓ A student considering **graphic design** can explore whether they need a **degree or if certifications + portfolio work are enough.**

3. Encourage Test Runs Before Committing

✓ **Before enrolling in a program**, see if they can **shadow a professional, do an internship, or take an introductory course.**

Example:

✓ If your teen wants to study **psychology**, they might first work as a **behavioral aide or volunteer in a counseling setting.**

4. Discuss Finances Openly

✓ Help them understand the **financial side of each path** – without fear or pressure.

Example Parent Dialogue:

✓ **Parent:** "Let's compare what college will cost and what kind of salary you can expect after graduation."

✓ **Teen:** "I didn't realize some degrees don't lead to high salaries."

✓ **Parent:** "Yeah, it's good to check that before taking on loans."

◆ **What's Next?**

Making an informed decision about **college, trade school, or going straight to work** isn't just about what sounds appealing – it's also about **understanding the financial realities of each path.**

In the next section, we'll explore:

✓ **The true cost of college and how to make it more affordable.**

✓ **Alternatives to traditional four-year programs that can still lead to great careers.**

✓ **Smart financial decisions teens (and parents) can make now to set them up for future success.**

✦ **Up Next: Understanding College Costs & Smart Financial Choices.**

📖 Section 7: Understanding College Costs & Smart Financial Choices

◆ **The Reality: College is Expensive – But There Are Options**

For many families, **college costs are one of the biggest concerns** when discussing career options.

      ✓ **Student loan debt is at an all-time high.**

      ✓ **Not every college degree leads to high-paying jobs.**

      ✓ **Many students don't realize all the ways to make college more affordable.**

☑ **Key Takeaway:** Instead of assuming **college is all or nothing,** parents and teens should explore **all the financial options available** to make a **smart, cost-effective decision.**

- **How to Help Your Teen Make a Financially Smart College Choice**

  - ✓ **Compare Costs Between Schools** – The price difference between **in-state vs. out-of-state, private vs. public, or community college vs. university** can be **huge.**

  - ✓ **Look for Schools That Offer the Best Aid** – Some expensive private schools **offer more scholarships than public ones.**

  - ✓ **Encourage Part-Time & Alternative Paths** – Some students **work while attending college part-time** to minimize debt.

  - ✓ **Consider Community College First** – Two years of community college before transferring can **save thousands of dollars.**

- **Example Cost Breakdown:**

A student attending **community college for 2 years, then transferring** to a state university **could save $20,000–$40,000** compared to four years at a university.

- **Other Ways to Reduce Costs:**

  - ✓ **Online Degree Programs** – Often more flexible & lower-cost.

  - ✓ **Employer Tuition Assistance** – Some companies will pay for a degree if you work there.

  - ✓ **Work-Study & Paid Internships** – Earn money while gaining experience.

◆ **Helping Your Teen Make a Smart Investment**

College is **only worth the cost if it leads to real opportunities.** Before choosing a school, help your teen research:

✓ **Starting salaries in their field** – Is the degree cost justified by potential earnings?

✓ **Debt-to-income ratio** – Will they be able to **comfortably pay off student loans?**

✓ **Alternative paths** – Would **trade school, bootcamps, or employer training** lead to the same career at a lower cost?

◆ **Example:**

• A **student wants to study psychology** but isn't sure if grad school is financially realistic. Instead of jumping into loans, they **work in an entry-level counseling role first** to test the field before committing to more education.

- **Final Thought: College is a Tool, Not a Requirement**

  ✓ College is a great option for many careers – but it's not the
  only path.

  ✓ Choosing a financially smart way to attend matters just as
  much as choosing the right major.

  ✓ Your teen's success isn't defined by a degree – it's defined by
  how they build their skills, experience, and opportunities.

* **What's Next?**

Now that we've explored **the different paths after high school,** let's take a closer look at **how to ensure your teen makes a financially smart decision.**

* **Up Next: Encouraging Growth Without Pressure.**

📖 Section 8: Encouraging Growth Without Pressure

Once your teen has explored their **strengths, interests, and career options**, the next challenge is **helping them move forward without making them feel rushed or overwhelmed.**

Many parents worry:

✓ *How do I encourage my teen to take action without making them feel like I'm forcing a decision?*

✓ *What if they aren't making progress or keep changing their mind?*

✓ *How do I help them stay motivated without adding too much pressure?*

The key is **supporting their growth while giving them the space to make their own choices.** You want to help them take **small steps toward their future** while keeping the door open for **change and discovery.**

◆ **The Balance Between Guidance and Independence**

Your teen **still needs your support,** but they also need the **freedom to make their own decisions.** Here's how to **strike that balance.**

◈ **1. Be a Sounding Board, Not a Dictator**

You want to help guide them, but **they need to feel ownership** over their future.

◈ **Example Parent Dialogue:**

  ✓ **Parent:** "I know this is a big decision, and I'm here to help you figure it out."

  ✓ **Teen:** "I just don't know where to start."

  ✓ **Parent:** "That's okay! Let's start small — what's one career or topic you'd like to learn more about?"

  ☑ *Why this works:* It makes the conversation **collaborative** instead of feeling like an **interrogation.**

◈ **2. Celebrate Effort, Not Just Results**

Progress isn't just about **choosing a career.** Even small steps — like researching a career, talking to a mentor, or taking a course — are **worth celebrating.**

✦ Example Parent Dialogue:

✓ **Parent:** "I noticed you looked up information about cybersecurity. That's awesome! What stood out to you?"

✓ **Teen:** "I didn't realize there were so many jobs in the field."

✓ **Parent:** "That's great! Want to check out a beginner course or job shadow someone in the industry?"

Why this works: It **encourages curiosity** without making them feel like they need all the answers immediately.

✦ 3. Encourage Curiosity Over Commitment

If your teen feels **paralyzed by the pressure to make a decision,** remind them that they **don't have to lock into one career path today.**

✦ Example Parent Dialogue:

✓ **Parent:** "Instead of picking a 'forever career,' what's something you'd like to explore right now?"

✓ **Teen:** "I like technology, but I'm not sure if I want to be a programmer."

✓ **Parent:** "That's okay! There are lots of careers in tech that don't require coding – let's see what else is out there."

Why this works: It **removes pressure** and shifts the focus to **exploration.**

◆ **Handling Setbacks, Indecision, and Self-Doubt**

Many teens **second-guess themselves** or feel stuck. Here's how to help them move forward.

◆ **1. Help Them Reframe Failure as Learning**

Some teens **avoid making decisions** because they're afraid of **choosing wrong.** Teach them that failure is **part of the process.**

◆ **Example Parent Dialogue:**

✓ **Teen:** "What if I pick the wrong career?"

✓ **Parent:** "That's completely normal! Most people try different things before they find the right fit. Every experience teaches you something useful."

Why this works: It **removes the fear of failure** and encourages them to **take action.**

◆ **2. Help Them See the Big Picture**

Sometimes, teens feel like they **should have everything figured out already.** Remind them that **careers evolve over time.**

◆ **Example Parent Dialogue:**

✓ **Parent:** "Careers aren't set in stone. Most adults switch jobs multiple times. You're just starting out, so it's okay to change directions later!"

☑ *Why this works:* It **eases the pressure** to make a **"perfect" choice** right now.

◆ **3. Let Them Experience Small Risks**

Teens learn best **through experience.** Give them space to **test out careers without high stakes.**

◆ **Example Parent Dialogue:**

✓ **Parent:** "I know you're curious about video editing. Want to take on a small project for fun and see how you like it?"

☑ *Why this works:* It **encourages action** without making it feel like a **huge decision.**

◆ Encouraging Growth Without Rushing

Helping your teen move forward **doesn't mean rushing them into a decision.** It means **giving them opportunities to explore** while reminding them they're **in control of their own future.**

◆ Final Parent Tips:

✓ Encourage **curiosity, not commitment.**

✓ Support **small steps and celebrate progress.**

✓ Give them space to **explore without fear of failure.**

◆ What's Next?

You've guided your teen through **career exploration** and **decision-making.** Now, how do you continue to support them **without hovering?**

◆ Up Next: Being Their Best Support System.

📖 Section 9:
Being Their Best Support System

Your teen is **stepping into the next phase of their life,** and while they may not have everything figured out yet, they **don't have to navigate it alone.**

Your role is shifting – from **decision-maker to supporter, from guide to trusted advisor.**

The best way to continue helping them? **Be available, be encouraging, and trust that they will figure things out in their own time.**

◆ How to Support Without Hovering

It can be tempting to **keep checking in, offering suggestions, or worrying if they seem unsure.** But real growth happens when teens feel **trusted to make their own choices.**

Here's how to **stay involved without micromanaging.**

◆ 1. Let Them Take Ownership

Your teen needs to feel that **their career journey belongs to them,** not just something you're managing for them.

◆ Example Parent Dialogue:

✓ **Parent:** "What's one small step you want to take toward your career goals this month?"

✓ **Teen:** "I guess I could reach out to someone in the field."

✓ **Parent:** "That sounds great! Do you want any help figuring out how to approach them, or do you feel good handling it on your own?"

☑ *Why this works:* It keeps **them in the driver's seat** while showing you're still there for support.

◆ 2. Offer Advice Only When Needed

Instead of jumping in with **solutions,** ask if they actually **want advice first.**

◆ Example Parent Dialogue:

✓ **Parent:** "Are you looking for advice, or do you just want to talk it out?"

✓ **Teen:** "I think I just need to vent for a minute."

✓ **Parent:** "Got it – go ahead, I'm listening."

Why this works: It makes them feel **heard** without feeling like they're being **pushed toward a decision.**

◆ 3. Celebrate Their Wins – Big and Small

Even if they haven't **landed their dream job yet,** every step forward is progress. Recognizing their effort helps **boost confidence** and keeps them motivated.

◆ Example Parent Dialogue:

✓ **Parent:** "I saw you updated your resume – nice job! That's a big step."

✓ **Teen:** "Yeah, I finally got around to it."

✓ **Parent:** "That's awesome! It's one of those things that's easy to put off, but now you're ready when opportunities come up."

☑ *Why this works:* It reinforces **progress over perfection.**

◆ Keeping the Conversation Open

Even as your teen becomes more independent, it's important to **keep communication flowing.** Here's how to check in without making it feel forced.

◆ 1. Make Career Talks a Natural Part of Everyday Life

Instead of **formal career check-ins**, weave career discussions into **casual moments.**

◆ Example Parent Dialogue:

✓ **At dinner:** "I read about a woman who started her own business in her 20s – want to hear how she did it?"

✓ **On a drive:** "I heard a podcast about the future of jobs in tech – thought you might find it interesting."

✓ **Watching TV:** "That character's job is interesting. What do you think it would be like to do something like that?"

Why this works: It makes career talk feel **casual and ongoing,** not like a high-pressure conversation.

◆ 2. Encourage a Growth Mindset

Teens who think **career success happens overnight** can get discouraged **when things don't go perfectly.** Teach them that **growth takes time.**

◆ Example Parent Dialogue:

✓ **Teen:** "I applied for an internship, but I didn't get it."

✓ **Parent:** "That's frustrating, but applying was a great step! Do you want to tweak your resume and try again somewhere else?"

☑ *Why this works:* It helps them see setbacks as **learning opportunities, not failures.**

◆ Letting Go: Trusting Their Path

At some point, you have to **trust that they will figure things out.** Your guidance is **invaluable,** but ultimately, they have to **take ownership of their journey.**

Here's how to support them **without stepping in too much.**

◆ 1. Resist the Urge to Overcorrect

Your teen will make choices you **might not have made.** That's okay. Ask yourself:

◆ *Is this about my fears, or their journey?*

✓ Instead of **correcting them immediately,** ask **why they're drawn to that path.**

◆ Example Parent Dialogue:

✓ **Parent:** "I noticed you're considering a career in video game development – what interests you about that field?"

✓ **Teen:** "I love the creative side of designing worlds and characters."

✓ **Parent:** "That's really cool! Have you looked into what skills you'd need to break into the industry?"

☑ *Why this works:* It **validates their interest** while guiding them to **think critically.**

2. Remember, Detours Are Normal

Most people don't have **a straight career path.** Remind your teen that **it's okay to change their mind.**

Example Parent Dialogue:

✓ **Teen:** "I thought I wanted to be a teacher, but now I'm not sure."

✓ **Parent:** "That's totally normal! What parts of it do you like, and what parts make you hesitate?"

Why this works: It **helps them reflect** instead of feeling like they're failing.

3. Your Support Means More Than Your Approval

Your teen may not **follow the exact path you envisioned,** but knowing they have your **support and belief** will give them the confidence to move forward.

Example Parent Dialogue:

✓ **Parent:** "No matter what you decide to do, I know you're going to find something that fits you."

Why this works: It reassures them that **your love and support aren't conditional on their career choices.**

Final Thought: You're Doing Better Than You Think

If you've made it this far, you **care deeply about your teen's future.** That alone makes a huge difference.

✦ **Reminder for Parents:**

✓ **You don't need to have all the answers.**

✓ **Your teen doesn't need a perfect plan — just a willingness to explore.**

✓ **Your role is to provide support, guidance, and encouragement.**

☑ **Key Takeaway:** The most valuable thing you can give them **is your belief in their ability to find their way.**

◆ **What's Next?**

Now that your teen is moving forward, how do you continue supporting them **without overstepping?**

✦ **Up Next: Conclusion — Trust the Process.**

📖 Conclusion:
Trust the Process

CAN'T I JUST HELP MY KID PICK A PATH?

Guiding your teen through career exploration **isn't about having all the answers** – it's about being a steady source of **support, encouragement, and perspective** as they figure things out for themselves.

If there's one thing to take away from this guide, it's this:

- ✓ **Your teen's journey will unfold in its own way and at its own pace.**

- ✓ **No career path is linear, and that's okay.**

- ✓ **Your role isn't to chart the entire course for them, but to walk beside them, offering guidance when they need it and space when they don't.**

- ◆ **Career Paths Are Not Straight Lines – And That's a Good Thing**

If you think about your own career journey, chances are it **wasn't a straight path from A to B.**

- ✓ You may have **changed jobs, industries, or even gone back to school** at some point.

- ✓ You may have discovered **unexpected opportunities** that shaped your future in ways you never anticipated.

- ✓ You may still be figuring out what you want to do – and that's okay!

The same will be true for your teen.

- ☑ **Key Takeaway:** Instead of worrying about whether they're making the **"right" decision**, trust that they will learn, grow, and adapt along the way.

◆ What If They Struggle or Change Their Mind?

It's **normal** for teens to start on one path and realize it's not quite right for them. This doesn't mean they **failed** – it means they're learning.

◆ Example:

✓ A teen who pursues **engineering** might later realize they prefer **teaching math.**

✓ A student who starts a **business degree** might find they love **graphic design and pivot into marketing.**

☑ How Parents Can Support Change:

✓ Remind them that **career shifts are normal** and not a sign of failure.

✓ Encourage them to **take the skills they've gained** and apply them to new opportunities.

✓ Help them see that **detours often lead to new strengths and discoveries.**

◆ Example Parent Dialogue:

✓ **Teen:** "I thought I wanted to do computer science, but I don't love coding."

✓ **Parent:** "That's completely okay! What parts of it did you enjoy? Maybe there's a career in tech that better fits your strengths."

☑ *Why this works:* It **keeps the conversation open** and reassures them that **exploring is part of the process.**

◆ Your Support Means More Than Your Advice

At the end of the day, **your teen's success won't come from you making the right decision for them – it will come from them learning to make decisions for themselves.**

What they need most from you **isn't a roadmap – it's belief in their ability to navigate the journey.**

✦ **The Most Valuable Things You Can Give Your Teen:**

✓ **Encouragement** – Let them know you believe in them, even if they're unsure of their path.

✓ **Patience** – Give them the space to explore and change directions if needed.

✓ **Perspective** – Remind them that success is about growth, not a perfect first decision.

☑ **Key Takeaway:** Your teen **will remember your support far more than any career advice you give.**

- **Actionable Next Steps for Parents**

Now that you've **helped your teen explore their future**, what can you do to keep supporting them **without overstepping?**

- **Here are three small but meaningful ways to stay involved:**

✓ **1. Check in occasionally — without pressure.**

> - *Example:* "I know you were looking into psychology careers — have you learned anything interesting?"

✓ **2. Celebrate small wins.**

> - Example: "I saw you signed up for that internship — that's awesome!"

✓ **3. Keep an open-door policy.**

> - Example: "No matter what, I'm always here if you want to talk about what's next."

Why this works: It **keeps communication open** without making them feel like they're being constantly evaluated.

◆ **Final Thought: You're Doing Better Than You Think**

By reading this book, you've shown that you **care deeply about your teen's future.** That alone makes a huge difference.

◆ **Reminder for Parents:**

✓ You don't need to have **all the answers.**

✓ Your teen doesn't need to make **a perfect choice today.**

✓ Your role is to **support, encourage, and trust that they will figure it out.**

Your belief in them **matters more than you realize.**

No matter where their journey takes them, they will **always have you in their corner.**

◆ **What's Next?**

There is no single **"right" path** for your teen – only the one that makes the most sense for them. **Trust their ability to figure it out.**

✓ **Keep the conversation open.**

✓ **Support their journey, even if it looks different from what you ex-pected.**

✓ **Remember that careers evolve, and there's no single perfect choice.**

Your teen is **lucky to have your support.** Now, it's time to let them explore, grow, and discover their own path – knowing that you'll always be in their corner.

☑ **You've done your part. Now, trust the process.**

What's Next?

This book was written as a companion to *Can't I Just Stay in My Room?*, a teen career guide for kids who'd rather not talk about it. If your child is still figuring things out (or actively avoiding the conversation), that's the place to start.

If college isn't part of the plan – or your teen closed the first book and still didn't want a dorm room – there's a follow-up just for them:

Can't I Just Skip College?

For Everyone Who Closed the First Book and Still Didn't Want a Dorm Room

You can find both books, along with bonus materials, at https://cantijust.com.

For Educators and Counselors

If you work with students, we've created educator-friendly versions of our tools.

Downloadable PowerPoint slides, printable workbooks, and teacher guides are available to support classroom or group use. Visit our For Schools page at cantijust.com to learn more.

Be Part of the Mission

Wayfinder exists to help young people build better futures—with confidence, clarity, and a little less panic. If this book helped you support your teen, we'd love it if you left a review on Amazon or shared it with someone else who needs it.

You can also follow us online for updates, new books, free resources, and a little encouragement when the road ahead feels uncertain.

We're glad you're here.

About the Author

Jennifer Larsen has a habit of turning big questions into clear, doable steps—and she's built a career around helping others do the same. With a background in education and psychology (and a low tolerance for boring advice), she has created this guide for anyone tired of being asked, "What do you want to be when you grow up?"—especially if they're already grown.